NAKED LADIES' LUNCHES

marina beebe

NAKED LADIES' LUNCHES

An Orgy of Eating

By Marina Beebe

GATEWAY BOOKS

San Francisco

Gateway Books
1750 Post Street—Suite 111
San Francisco, CA 94115

Editors: Margaret Russell and Barbara D'Arcy
Editorial Coordinator: Judith Merwin
Text Design: José Barbosa
Cover Design: James Lohse

Library of Congress Cataloging-in-Publication Data

Beebe, Marina, 1938—
    Naked ladies' lunches.

    Includes index.
    1. Cookery.   2. Luncheons   I. Title
TX715.B412   1987   641.5   86-33604
ISBN 0-933469-01-2 (pbk.)

By *way of introduction to*
Naked Ladies' Lunches ❧

Do Naked Ladies really need an introduction?
By a man? Well, why not? I can't say I was there but only that
these drawings make me wish I had been. For the food as well
as for the women, not to mention the naked men and children
who sometimes were allowed to sneak in. But let us concen-
trate on the art. Is it a tribute to the artist to say I don't
recognize any of them with their clothes off? A line drawing
can only go so far, only as far as the artist allows it to go.
It takes oil paint to get the soul. And, after all, she was
busy eating . . . .

Lawrence Ferlinghetti
June, 1986

Artist's Foreword

This book, based on my journal, depicts our meetings at each other's houses where we took turns modeling and drawing and then partook of the gustatory splendor— those delicious lunches. Sometimes we were joined by kids, husbands or boyfriends; mostly it was just the women.

All of this I recorded to the accompaniment of, "Hurry up and draw it so we can eat!"

We are dedicated artists. Feminist? Well, we are all independent, ferocious about or protective of our precious freedom. Artists are outlaws, and if we broke some rules, through this we created new ones.

Marina Beebe

Acknowledgements

What started as a sketch book of life drawings and a journal of memorable meals, would not have come together as a comprehensible work without the perseverence and attention to detail of Margaret Russell and Barbara D'Arcy. Of course, without the cooperation of all the naked ladies themselves, there would have been neither any life drawing sessions nor any occasions for us to gather on a weekly basis.
I am delighted to share the journal with you.

Marina Beebe

LUNCHES

To Lee Adair Hastings who taught me to draw from life

COLD BORSCHT   ON A HOT DAY

PUT 4 C JELLIED BEEF CONSOMMÉ
INTO A BOWL. ADD 4 SEEDED
CHOPPED TOMATOES & 4 COOKED
BEETS CUT UP, 2 T MINCED
PARSLEY & 4 GREEN ONIONS
FINELY CHOPPED. STIR AND
LEAVE IN REFRIGERATOR 2 HOURS
BEFORE SERVING. IF DESIRED,
SERVE WITH SOUR CREAM.

SERVES 4.

GRAPE LEAVES STUFFED   BY MIMI

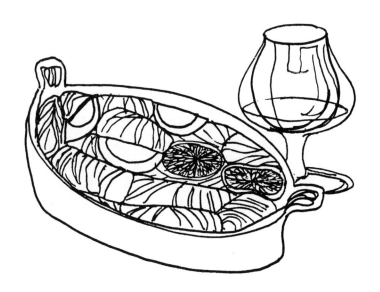

STUFFING

1 LARGE YELLOW ONION, CHOPPED
3/4 LB. GROUND LAMB
1 C RICE, PARTIALLY COOKED
3 T CURRANTS
3 T PINE NUTS
1/2 t GROUND CUMIN
2 T CHOPPED PARSLEY

1 QUART JAR GRAPE LEAVES, RINSED
2 C CHICKEN BROTH

SAUTÉ ONIONS TILL SOFT. ADD
LAMB & COOK TILL LAMB ISN'T
PINK. MIX WITH ALL OTHER
STUFFING INGREDIENTS & PUT
1 T STUFFING ON EACH GRAPE
LEAF. FOLD INTO NEAT PACK —
AGE. BAKE AT 350° IN THE
BROTH IN A COVERED CASSEROLE
FOR ABOUT ½ HOUR.

SERVES 8.

AND A CAKE

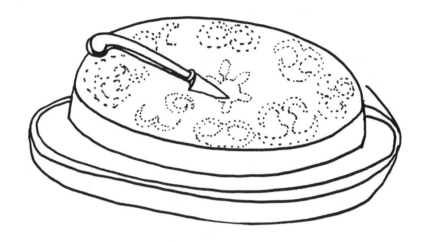

½ C BUTTER
1 C SUGAR OR HONEY
2 ¼ C FLOUR
½ t SALT
1 EGG LIGHTLY BEATEN
½ C MILK
½ C ORANGE JUICE
1 t BAKING SODA IN ¼ C HOT WATER
GRATED RIND OF 2 LARGE ORANGES
1 C CHOPPED WALNUTS OR PECANS
1 C CHOPPED DATES

CREAM BUTTER & SUGAR OR HONEY.
BEAT IN ALL OTHER INGREDIENTS,
ALTERNATING DRY WITH LIQUID.
ADD RIND, NUTS & DATES LAST.
BAKE AT 350° IN A BUTTERED,
FLOURED, 9" CAKE PAN FOR ABOUT
I HOUR. COOL & TURN OUT BOTTOM
SIDE UP ONTO A PLATE. TO
DECORATE, CUT OUT A (FAIRLY
LARGE) DESIGN ON A ROUND
PIECE OF PAPER. COVER CAKE &
SPRINKLE POWDERED SUGAR OVER
IT. REMOVE STENCIL CAREFULLY.

LUNCH AT KAREN'S

CONSUMMATED CONSOMMÉ

TO 4 CANS OF CONSOMMÉ ADD
2 6 OZ. JARS OF MARINATED
ARTICHOKE HEARTS CUT IN
SLIVERS, & 1 15 OZ. CAN OF
GARBANZO BEANS. MIX ALL
TOGETHER WITH JUICE OF 4
LEMONS & A HANDFUL OF
CHOPPED PARSLEY. CHILL.

SERVES 6.

CUCUMBER SALAD

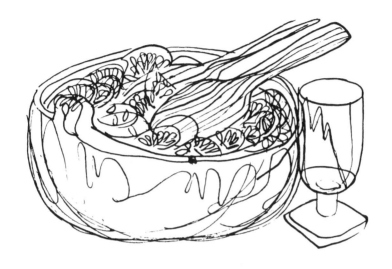

4 MEDIUM CUCUMBERS
1 LARGE GARLIC CLOVE CRUSHED
S & P
4 T SOUR CREAM OR MORE
1 t SUGAR
1 t WINE VINEGAR
PAPRIKA — GENEROUS AMOUNT

PEEL CUCUMBER AND SLICE PAPER
THIN. PLACE IN BOWL AND SPRINKLE
WITH SALT. REFRIGERATE 1 HOUR.
WASH THOROUGHLY WITH COLD
WATER AND SQUEEZE DRY. ADD
OTHER INGREDIENTS. SPRINKLE
WITH LOTS OF PAPRIKA. CHILL
AND SERVE.

SERVES 4 – 6.

CRÊPES

2 EGGS
2/3 C FLOUR
1 C MILK
1/3 CUBE MELTED SWEET BUTTER
PINCH OF SALT
1 t SUGAR (ADD FOR DESSERT FILL-
   ING ONLY)

PUT ALL INGREDIENTS IN BLENDER
& MIX AT HIGH SPEED OR MIX WITH
ELECTRIC BEATER. LET BATTER
STAND FOR 30 MINUTES. COOK
EACH CRÊPE IN PAN WITH MELTED
BUTTER BY COATING PAN WITH ONE
LADLE FULL OF BATTER. CAREFULLY
TURN CRÊPE WHEN TOP IS SET.
BROWN OTHER SIDE FOR ABOUT
30 SECONDS.

MAKES 12.

FILLINGS:

SPINACH
4 10 OZ. PACKAGES FROZEN, CHOPPED
  SPINACH
5 T BUTTER
1 ONION FINELY CHOPPED
NUTMEG TO TASTE
S & P
1/2 C SOUR CREAM
1/4 C HALF & HALF
6 T MADEIRA OR SHERRY

COOK SPINACH ACCORDING TO DIREC-
TIONS ON PACKAGE. SQUEEZE DRY
& CHOP VERY FINE. RETURN TO PAN
& ADD BUTTER, S & P, NUTMEG. ADD
ONION TO SPINACH MIXTURE & COOK
BRIEFLY. THEN ADD REMAINING
INGREDIENTS.

CHICKEN
3 T BUTTER
3 T GREEN ONION, MINCED WITH
  GREENS
1 t DRIED OREGANO, CRUMBLED
1 C SLICED MUSHROOMS
1/2 C DRY VERMOUTH
1 C SOUR CREAM
3 C COOKED CHICKEN, CUBED

SAUTÉ VEGETABLES & OREGANO
IN BUTTER FOR A FEW MINUTES.
ADD WINE & SIMMER TILL WINE
REDUCES BY HALF. STIR IN
SOUR CREAM, THEN CHICKEN.
FILL 12 6" CRÊPES WITH ¼ C
CHICKEN EACH. PUT ROLLED
CRÊPES IN BUTTERED CASSEROLE.
COVER WITH FOIL & HEAT IN
350° OVEN.

COTTAGE CHEESE

8 OZ. SMALL CURD COTTAGE CHEESE
1 EGG - SEPARATED
3 T SOUR CREAM
SUGAR TO TASTE
GRATED RIND OF 2 LARGE LEMONS
HANDFUL OF RAISINS

FORCE COTTAGE CHEESE THROUGH
FINE SIEVE. MIX IN EGG YOLK, SOUR
CREAM, SUGAR, LEMON RIND & RAI-
SINS. BEAT EGG WHITE TILL STIFF
& FOLD IN.

FILLS 12 CRÊPES.

SERVES 6.

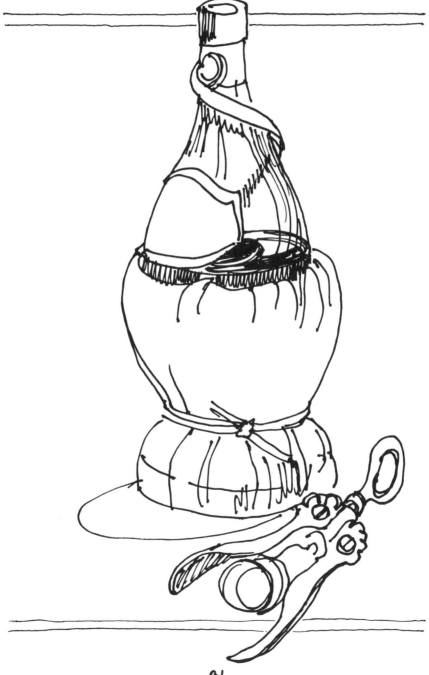

MUSHROOMS MERVEILLEUX

2 T BUTTER
1 MEDIUM ONION, CHOPPED
1½ LBS. MUSHROOMS, SLICED
1 t PAPRIKA
½ t MARJORAM
½ t TARRAGON
1 t LEMON JUICE
1/4 C SHERRY
1 C SOUR CREAM
S & P
4-6 SLICES GRILLED CANADIAN
  BACON OR HAM
4-6 ENGLISH MUFFIN HALVES,
  TOASTED
MINCED PARSLEY

SAUTÉ ONION IN BUTTER. ADD
MUSHROOMS, S & P, HERBS, LEMON
JUICE & SHERRY. STIR IN SOUR
CREAM & HEAT GENTLY. TOP
ENGLISH MUFFIN HALVES WITH
CANADIAN BACON, THEN MUSH-
ROOM MIXTURE. SPRINKLE
PARSLEY OVER ALL.

SERVES 4-6.

PINEAPPLE WITH AVOCADO

and a marvelous
fruit salad made
by Jill, the recipe
for which is on the
following page ⟶

SIMPLY HALVE A RIPE PINE-
APPLE; REMOVE CORE; CARE-
FULLY CUT OUT THE FRUIT
AND CUT INTO CHUNKS.
COMBINE WITH PIECES OF
2 AVOCADOS AND JUICE OF
2 LEMONS. ADD 2 OZ. OF
COINTREAU AND REFRIGERATE
TILL THOROUGHLY CHILLED.
GARNISH WITH FRESH MINT.

SERVES 6.

CHOCOLATE BARS

½ STICK SWEET BUTTER
    MELT IN LARGE FLAT PAN
1 C GRAHAM CRACKER
        CRUMBS   } SPRINKLE
1 C COCONUT   ON IN
6 OZ. CHOCOLATE CHIPS   ORDER
1 C SLIVERED ALMONDS   GIVEN

1 CAN CONDENSED SWEETENED
MILK DRIZZLED OVER
LAYERS OF ABOVE INGRE-
DIENTS

BAKE AT 350° FOR ABOUT
30 MINUTES. CUT INTO
SQUARES WHILE STILL WARM.

AFTER LUNCH XENIA MODELED

Outside the sun was warm and inside everybody was busy. The coffee dripped in the kitchen.

SPINACH SOUP

2 T BUTTER
2-3 CLOVES GARLIC, CRUSHED
3 GREEN ONIONS, CHOPPED WITH
  TOPS
1 T CHOPPED PARSLEY
1 t EACH MARJORAM, THYME, BASIL

COOK THIS 5 MINUTES & ADD

2/3 LB. CHOPPED SPINACH OR
  1 PACKAGE FROZEN DRAINED
  SPINACH, FINELY CHOPPED
3 C BROTH
S & P

SIMMER TOGETHER FOR A FEW
MINUTES. PURÉE IN BLENDER
& REHEAT. POUR INTO SOUP PLATES.
HEAT 1 C CREAM & SWIRL INTO
SOUP FOR MARBLEIZED EFFECT.

SERVES 4.

QUESADILLAS

12 CORN TORTILLAS
1 LB. MONTEREY JACK CHEESE
    (OR OTHER FAVORITE)
2 t SALSA JALAPEÑA (GREEN
    CHILE SAUCE)
COOKING OIL

PUT A LITTLE MORE THAN 1 OZ.
OF CHEESE IN MIDDLE OF CORN
(FLOUR IF YOU PREFER) TORTILLA.
ADD THE SALSA. FOLD TORTILLA
IN HALF. FRY IN A HOT IRON
SKILLET OR ON GRIDDLE WHICH
HAS BEEN BRUSHED WITH OIL
FOR ABOUT 2 MINUTES ON EACH
SIDE TILL TORTILLA IS LIGHTLY
BROWNED AND CHEESE MELTED.

SERVES 6

STRAWBERRY SHORTCAKE

2 C FLOUR
2 T BAKING POWDER
1 t SALT
1 T SUGAR (OR 1 T HONEY)
1/2 STICK BUTTER
1/2 C MILK + -

WITH YOUR FINGERS MIX THE
BUTTER INTO ALL THE DRY
STUFF. THEN ADD THE MILK
& KNEAD QUICKLY, PAT INTO
A FLAT SHAPE, CUT INTO
ROUNDS WITH A GLASS; BAKE
AT 450° FOR 10 MINUTES.
SPLIT & FILL WITH STRAWBER-
RIES & YOGURT.

41

42

AT SUPER'S 12 JUNE

CREAM OF ASPARAGUS SOUP

1 BUNCH ASPARAGUS
1 QT. MILK
2 CUBES VEGETABLE BROTH
2 T BUTTER
2 T FLOUR

SIMMER ASPARAGUS IN MILK
WITH BROTH 5 MINUTES.
BLEND, RESERVING TIPS OF
ASPARAGUS FOR GARNISH.
STIR BUTTER WITH FLOUR IN
A HEAVY PAN. ADD BLENDED
ASPARAGUS BROTH TO BUTTER-
FLOUR ROUX, A LITTLE AT A
TIME, STIR TO THICKEN.
GARNISH & SERVE.
SERVES 4-6.

VERY GOOD CHICKEN SALAD

4 C COOKED CHICKEN CUT INTO
   LARGE PIECES
1 C CELERY CUT ON ANGLE INTO
   BIG CHUNKS
1 C MINCED GREEN PEPPER

DRESSING
2/3 C MAYONNAISE
1/4 C HALF & HALF
3 T BALSAMIC VINEGAR
S & P

PUT CHICKEN & VEGETABLES
INTO LARGE BOWL. MIX DRESSING
INGREDIENTS & TOSS WITH
CHICKEN. MAKE AHEAD.

SERVES 4−6.

CHEESECAKE

2 PT. RICOTTA OR SMALL CURD
  COTTAGE CHEESE
5 EGG YOLKS
1/8 LB. MELTED BUTTER
1/2 PT. SOUR CREAM
1/2 C HONEY
1 T VANILLA
2 T GRATED LEMON RIND

BLEND ALL OF THE INGREDIENTS.
POUR INTO A GRAHAM CRACKER
CRUST: 22 CRUSHED CRACKERS
(2 PKGS.) MIXED WITH A STICK
OF MELTED BUTTER, PRESSED
INTO A PAN. BAKE AT 350° 1 HOUR.

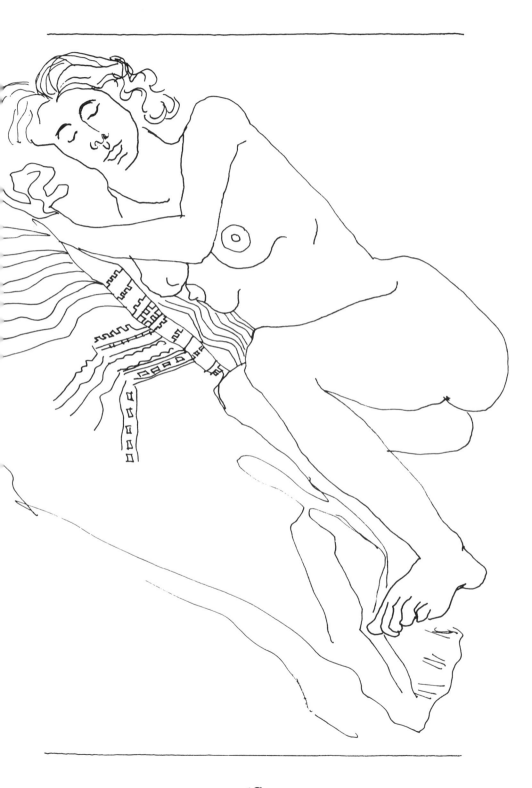

47

VEGETABLE SALAD

and it was so good that
I ate the rest of it.....

TOSS SLICED RADISHES, RED
CABBAGE, ZUCCINI, MUSHROOMS,
TOMATOES. ADD PEAS, KIDNEY
BEANS, CAULIFLOWER FLOWERETS.

It was all put together with
homemade mayonnaise.

MAYONNAISE

1 EGG
1 C OIL
1 t DIJON MUSTARD
2 T VINEGAR
SALT TO TASTE
} AT ROOM TEMP-ERATURE

BEAT EGG & SEASONINGS & ¼ C
OF THE OIL IN THE BLENDER.
THEN BEGIN ADDING THE REST
OF THE OIL DROP BY DROP BEAT-
ING AT HIGH SPEED TILL THE
MIXTURE "TAKES". CONTINUE
ADDING OIL SLOWLY UNTIL
THICK.

MAKES MORE THAN 1 C.

BROILED SANDWICHES

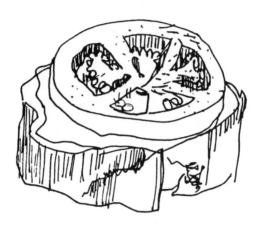

SLICED TOMATOES
SLICED CHEESE
SLICED FRENCH BREAD

HEAT IN BROILER TILL CHEESE
MELTS. SPRINKLE DILL ON TOP.

STRAWBERRY SQUISH

MAKE A GRAHAM CRACKER
CRUST IN A 9" PIE TIN.

PUT IN BLENDER:

½ LARGE PACKAGE CREAM CHEESE
1 CAN EAGLE BRAND CONDENSED
    MILK (14 OZ.)
½ C LEMON JUICE
½ PINT BASKET FRESH STRAW-
    BERRIES

POUR INTO CRUST; CHILL TILL
FIRM. GARNISH WITH REMAINDER
OF STRAWBERRIES.

SAUCE

SQUISH 1 PINT FRESH STRAW-
BERRIES IN BLENDER. SWEET-
EN WITH 2 TO 3 T POWDERED
SUGAR. (MAKES 1½ C.) SERVE
SEPARATELY IN A PITCHER.

LUNCH AT JILL AND AL'S   26 JUNE

POTAGE VELOUTÉ AUX CHAMPIGNONS

CHAMPIGNONS

4 T BUTTER
1½ LBS. MUSHROOMS, SLICED
   (RESERVE 6 WHOLE CAPS FOR GAR-
   NISH. SLIT IN 6 PLACES TO MAKE
   A FLOWER SHAPE.)
SPRINKLING OF FRESH HERBS CHOPPED
   (PARSLEY, CHIVES, MARJORAM)
S & P TO TASTE

IN A FRYING, PAN MELT BUTTER;
THEN SAUTÉ MUSHROOM SLICES &
CAPS. ADD HERBS; S & P. SET
CAPS ASIDE.

POTAGE

1/3 C BUTTER
1/3 C FLOUR
4 C STOCK (CHICKEN OR BEEF)
S & P TO TASTE
DASH OF CAYENNE PEPPER
1/2 C HEAVY CREAM

MELT BUTTER IN SAUCE PAN; ADD
FLOUR STIRRING INTO A SMOOTH
PASTE. SLOWLY POUR IN STOCK,
WHISKING UNTIL THICKENED &
SMOOTH. ADD CREAM, S & P &
CAYENNE. COMBINE MUSHROOM
MIXTURE WITH THE VELOUTÉ.
SERVE HOT FROM A TUREEN GAR-
NISHED WITH MUSHROOM CAPS &
MORE CHOPPED HERBS.

SERVES 6.

ham burgers

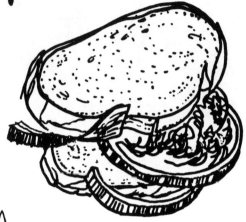

DEVILED HAM

1 LB. COOKED HAM
1/3 C SWEET PICKLE RELISH
1/3 C MAYONNAISE
1/4 C DIJON MUSTARD

GARLIC BREAD

1 LARGE LOAF FRENCH BREAD
1/8 LB. SOFT SWEET BUTTER
2 OR MORE CLOVES GARLIC, MASHED

MINCE HAM IN BLENDER OR
FOOD PROCESSOR. REMOVE & MIX
WITH RELISH, MAYONNAISE &
MUSTARD.

MEANWHILE, PREHEAT OVEN TO
450°. SLICE LOAF THROUGH &
SPREAD WITH GARLIC BUTTER.
HEAT TILL BUTTER MELTS INTO
BREAD; THEN FILL BETWEEN
SLICES WITH DEVILED HAM. CUT
INTO SANDWICHES AND SERVE
WITH RED ONION RINGS &
LETTUCE.

MAKES ABOUT 8 SANDWICHES.

When it's summertime, there are
lots of kids around, too.

APRICOT CLAFOUTI

4 EGGS, LIGHTLY BEATEN
1 C FLOUR
2 C WARM MILK
3/4 C SUGAR
2 T MELTED BUTTER
2 T BRANDY
PINCH OF SALT

1 LB. RIPE APRICOTS

GRADUALLY STIR FLOUR INTO BEATEN
EGGS. WHEN MIXTURE IS SMOOTH,
BEAT IN MILK, SUGAR, MELTED
BUTTER, BRANDY, & PINCH OF SALT.
POUR THIN LAYER OF BATTER INTO
BOTTOM OF WELL BUTTERED, SHALLOW
BAKING DISH & BAKE A FEW MINUTES
IN OVEN PREHEATED AT 425° TILL
IT BEGINS TO SET. THEN ARRANGE
PITTED APRICOT HALVES ON BATTER.
POUR REST OF BATTER OVER THEM.
REDUCE OVEN HEAT TO 400° & BAKE
30 TO 35 MINUTES TILL GOLDEN
BROWN & SLIGHTLY PUFFED.

SERVES 6 - 8

TOP

CORN SOUFFLÉ

4 EARS OF CORN
2 T BUTTER
2 T FLOUR
1 C ½ & ½
4 EGGS

PREHEAT OVEN TO 450°.
BUTTER & FLOUR SOUFFLÉ
DISH. CUT THE KERNELS OFF,
THE 4 EARS OF CORN. SAUTÉ
IN 2 T BUTTER OVER LOW
FLAME. ADD ½ & ½, STIR.
SEPARATE 4 EGGS. ADD THE
YOLKS TO THE CORN, STIRRING
IN EACH ONE. BEAT THE 4 WHITES
TILL THEY STAND UP, & FOLD
INTO CORN. POUR INTO SOUFFLÉ
DISH & BAKE 30 MINUTES.

SERVES 4.

The End of a Perfect Soufflé

PEAS AND SHRIMP SALAD

1 BUNCH WATERCRESS
1 PACK FROZEN PEAS
½ LB. COOKED SHRIMP
1 CAN WATER CHESTNUTS

BOUND WITH MAYONNAISE.
(MAYONNAISE IS AN EMUL-
SION AND WILL SUCCEED
IF ALL INGREDIENTS ARE
AT THE SAME TEMPERA-
TURE.)

1 EGG YOLK   BEAT
1 t DIJON MUSTARD   ALL
                    IN A
1 LEMON, JUICED   BOWL
1 CLOVE GARLIC   ADD
   optional   OIL

1 USE A WHISK AND
ADD OLIVE OIL (ABOUT
1 C) UNTIL IT EMULSI-
FIES.
ARRANGE PEAS, SHRIMP,
WATERCHESTNUTS ON A
BED OF WATERCRESS.

SERVES 6.

VANILLA BAVARIAN CREAM

1 ENVELOPE GELATIN
2 T COLD WATER
4 EGG YOLKS LIGHTLY BEATEN
1/2 C SUGAR
VANILLA BEAN
1 C WHIPPING CREAM

SOFTEN GELATIN IN WATER. COM-
BINE BEATEN EGG YOLKS WITH
SUGAR, STIRRING TILL SMOOTH &
CREAMY. SCALD MILK WITH VAN-
ILLA BEAN. REMOVE BEAN AND
POUR MILK SLOWLY INTO EGG
MIXTURE BEATING WITH WOODEN
SPOON. COOK MIXTURE OVER BOIL-
ING WATER WHISKING BRISKLY
UNTIL THICK. ADD SOFTENED
GELATIN & CONTINUE STIRRING
TILL DISSOLVED. COOL, STIRRING
EVERY SO OFTEN TO PREVENT
SKIN FROM FORMING. FINALLY,
FOLD IN CREAM, WHIPPED STIFF.
SPOON INTO GLASSES & CHILL.

SERVES 4

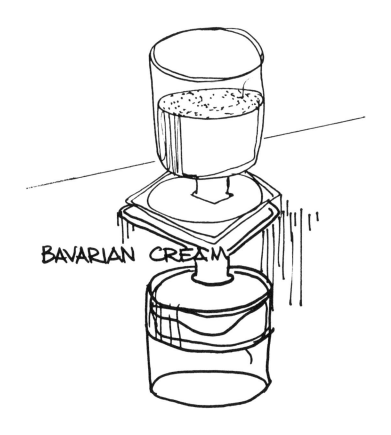

BAVARIAN CREAM

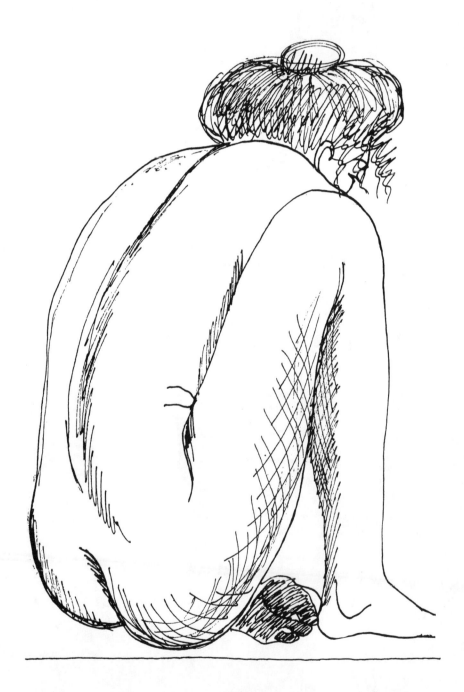

VEGETABLE FRITTATA

2 MEDIUM SIZED POTATOES,
   PARBOILED & SLICED
3 MEDIUM ZUCCINI, SLICED
1 ONION, SLICED
1 YELLOW PEPPER } CUT IN STRIPS
1 RED PEPPER
8 EGGS LIGHTLY BEATEN
1 C FRESHLY GRATED ASIAGO OR
   PARMESAN CHEESE
2 T CHOPPED FRESH ROSEMARY
S & P
BUTTER

SAUTÉ VEGETABLES WITH LOTS OF
BUTTER IN A HEAVY 10" FRYING
PAN, STARTING WITH THE ONION
& POTATOES. MIX BEATEN EGGS
WITH GRATED CHEESE, ROSEMARY,
S & P. SPOON WARM VEGETABLES
INTO EGG MIXTURE, STIRRING TO
PREVENT EGG FROM COOKING.
SCRAPE PAN FREE OF ANY VEGE-
TABLE BITS & BUBBLE MORE
BUTTER INTO IT. POUR IN FRITTATA
MIXTURE; COOK OVER MEDIUM
HEAT. AS EGGS SET, TIP PAN,
MOVING SET EGGS ASIDE WITH
SPATULA TO LET UNCOOKED EGG
RUN UNDERNEATH. BROWN TOP
UNDER BROILER & TURN OUT
ONTO PLATTER. SERVES 4 – 6.

FLAT BREAD

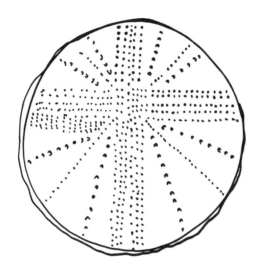

2 C BARLEY OR RYE FLOUR
½ t SALT
1 T SUGAR
2 t BAKING POWDER

1 C MILK OR CREAM
2 T MELTED BUTTER

MIX DRY INGREDIENTS. ADD
WET ONES. PUT DOUGH ON
BUTTERED COOKIE SHEET. PAT
INTO CIRCLE ABOUT 12" IN
DIAMETER BY ¼" THICK. MAKE
DESIGNS BY PRICKING ALL
OVER WITH A FORK. BAKE AT
450° FOR 10 MINUTES.

APPLE SAUCE TART

SESAME SEED CRUST

3/4 C WHOLEWHEAT FLOUR
1/4 C WHITE FLOUR
1 STICK BUTTER
1/8 C ICE WATER
3 T SESAME SEEDS
3 T HONEY

FOR EACH PIE MAKE THIS
CRUST RIGHT IN THE PAN.
BLEND ALL INGREDIENTS,
EXCEPT WATER & HONEY,
WITH FINGERTIPS, UNTIL
MIXTURE RESEMBLES FINE
MEAL. ADD WATER & HONEY;
FORM DOUGH INTO BALL.
PAT OUT WITH FINGERS. FILL.

FILLING

1 14 OZ. CAN APPLESAUCE
1 14 OZ. CAN SWEETENED
        CONDENSED MILK
4 EGG YOLKS LIGHTLY BEATEN
1/2 C LEMON JUICE
GRATED RIND OF 2 LARGE
        LEMONS

MIX TOGETHER & FOLD IN

4 EGG WHITES, BEATEN UNTIL
        STIFF

POUR INTO CRUST. BAKE AT
350° FOR 40 MINUTES, OR
UNTIL TOP IS LIGHTLY BROWNED.

MAKES 2 9" TARTS.

LUNCH AT LEE'S   24 JULY

SHRIMP IN SOUR CREAM

2 T BUTTER
2 CLOVES GARLIC, CRUSHED
3 GREEN ONIONS, CHOPPED
   WITH TOPS
1 LB. RAW SHRIMP, SHELLED &
   CLEANED
DASH OF TABASCO SAUCE
S & P
1 C WHITE WINE
1 C SOUR CREAM

BROWN GARLIC IN BUTTER.
ADD GREEN ONIONS, SHRIMP &
SEASONINGS. STIR & SAUTÉ
TILL SHRIMP TURNS PINK.
POUR IN WINE; SIMMER A
FEW MINUTES TILL WINE IS
REDUCED BY HALF. ADD SOUR
CREAM, STIRRING TILL SAUCE
IS SMOOTH. SERVE WITH BROWN
RICE.

SERVES 4.

AVOCADO, ROMAINE & CUCUMBER SALAD

MAKE A NEST OF ROMAINE
LETTUCE LEAVES. ON IT
ARRANGE AVOCADO SLICES
AND CUCUMBER SLICES.
DRESS WITH
2T VINEGAR
6T OLIVE OIL
1 t DIJON MUSTARD
1 CLOVE GARLIC, CRUSHED
BLEND ALL INGREDIENTS
WITH A WHISK.

FRESH PEACH PIE

SHORT CRUST PASTRY

4 OZ. SWEET BUTTER, FROZEN
5 OZ. UNBLEACHED FLOUR, CHILLED
1 – 1½ T ICED WATER
1 T SUGAR
PINCH OF SALT

COARSELY GRATE FROZEN BUTTER
INTO FLOUR. THEN RUB TOGETHER
WITH FINGER TIPS TILL MIXTURE
LOOKS LIKE CORNMEAL. SPRINKLE
WATER EVENLY OVER THIS &
GENTLY PRESS TOGETHER, GATHER-
ING UP ALL THE CRUMBS. ROLL
FROM CENTER OUT ON A FLOURED
BOARD TILL CRUST IS ⅛" THICK.
LINE 9" PIE TIN WITH THE CRUST;
PRICK WELL WITH FORK AROUND
BOTTOM & SIDES. BAKE IN OVEN
PREHEATED TO 425° UNTIL GOLD-
EN BROWN, ABOUT 15 MINUTES.

FILLING

1 C SUGAR
1 C WATER
1 T CORNSTARCH
FRESH GRATED NUTMEG & LEMON
   JUICE TO TASTE
6 LARGE RIPE PEACHES

COMBINE FIRST 5 INGREDIENTS
IN SAUCEPAN. COOK & STIR TILL
SUGAR MELTS & SYRUP IS THICK.
COOL. PEEL PEACHES & SLICE
INTO SYRUP. POUR FILLING INTO
PASTRY SHELL. TOP WITH WHIP-
PED CREAM LIGHTLY FLAVORED
WITH VANILLA.

MEXICAN LUNCH AT MIMI'S   31 JULY

CHILE CON QUESO APPETIZER

½ C CHOPPED ONION
1 CLOVE GARLIC
OIL
1 TOMATO, CHOPPED
1 4 OZ. CAN CHOPPED GREEN
  CHILES
1½ C GRATED JACK CHEESE

SAUTÉ ONION & GARLIC IN OIL,
ADD CHILES & TOMATO. SIMMER
A FEW MINUTES. (ADD WATER
IF MIXTURE THICKENS TOO
MUCH.) ADD CHEESE & CON-
TINUE COOKING SLOWLY TILL
CHEESE MELTS. SERVE WITH
TOSTADITAS.

TOSTADITAS (TORTILLA CHIPS)

CUT A DOZEN 6 INCH CORN
TORTILLAS INTO 8 WEDGES EACH.
DEEP FRY IN 3 BATCHES UNTIL
CRISP & GOLDEN. DRAIN ON
PAPER TOWEL; THEN SHAKE IN
A PAPER BAG WITH ½ t SALT.
SERVE WITH SALSA OR GUACAMOLE.

GUACAMOLE

3 AVOCADOS, MASHED
2 CLOVES GARLIC } FINELY
1/2 C ONION } CHOPPED
JUICE OF 1 LEMON
1/4 C SALSA, RED OR GREEN

COMBINE ALL INGREDIENTS.
GARNISH WITH COARSELY
GRATED CHEDDAR OR JACK
CHEESE & CHOPPED BLACK
OLIVES.

MEXICAN BLACK BEANS

SOAK 1 LB. OF BLACK BEANS
OVERNIGHT. BOIL IN 6 C WATER
FOR 1 HOUR. ADD 1 MEDIUM
ONION, CHOPPED, 3 STALKS OF
CELERY, CHOPPED, 1/4 t RED
PEPPER FLAKES, S & P. COOK
UNTIL BEANS ARE SOFT (ABOUT
2 HOURS OR MORE). SERVE WITH
RICE & TORTILLA CHIPS.

MEXICAN BEEF STEW

2 LBS. BONED CHUCK
1 C CARROTS   } CUBED
2 LARGE POTATOES
1 C FINELY CHOPPED ONIONS
3 CLOVES GARLIC
1 C GREEN CHILE SALSA
2 TOMATOES, PEELED & CHOPPED

SAUTÉ EACH ABOVE INGREDIENT SEPARATELY, ONE BY ONE IN PAN, EXCEPT TOMATOES, ENDING WITH SALSA. RETURN EVERY—THING TO POT & SIMMER COVER—ED FOR 15 MINUTES. SALT TO TASTE. CONTINUE COOKING UNTIL MEAT IS FORK TENDER, ABOUT 45 MINUTES, ADDING TOMATOES LAST 15 MINUTES. SERVE WITH BEANS, SPANISH RICE & FLOUR TORTILLAS.

THIS LUNCH SERVES 6.

PURÉED POTATO SOUP

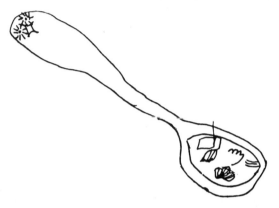

1 t GROUND TURMERIC
1 t MUSTARD SEEDS
1 t CUMIN SEEDS
1 t GROUND CORIANDER
1 t DRIED SWEET BASIL LEAVES
  OR 8 FRESH LEAVES, CHOPPED
4 T BUTTER
1 LARGE ONION, DICED
3 C POTATOES, DICED
2 CLOVES GARLIC, CRUSHED
4 C CHICKEN BROTH
1 C HEAVY CREAM
½ C YOGURT

SAUTÉ THE SPICES &
HERBS IN BUTTER. WHEN
THE MUSTARD SEEDS ARE
JUMPING AROUND IN
THE FRYING PAN, ADD
ONION & GARLIC. COOK
TILL ONION IS TRANS-
PARENT; THEN STIR
IN THE POTATOES.

COVER ALL WITH CHICKEN BROTH.

SIMMER FOR ½ HOUR. COOL SLIGHT-
LY & PURÉE IN BLENDER, ADDING THE
CREAM & YOGURT. CHILL THOROUGHLY
OR SERVE HOT. BEFORE SERVING,
SWIRL IN A HANDFUL OF CHOPPED
FRESH CORIANDER OR PARSLEY.

SERVES 8.

LENTIL SALAD

1 12 OZ. PACKAGE LENTILS,
  COOKED
1 RED PEPPER
1 GREEN PEPPER } MINCED
1 RED ONION
1 LARGE CARROT

2 C JICAMA OR WATER CHEST-
  NUTS, CUBED
2/3 C RICE VINEGAR
S & FRESHLY GROUND P
LOTS OF CHOPPED PARSLEY

MIX ALL BUT PARSLEY TOGETH-
ER. MARINATE IN REFRIGERA-
TOR FOR SEVERAL HOURS.
TOSS IN PARSLEY & SERVE ON
INDIVIDUAL PLATES DECORATED
WITH A SPRIG OF PARSLEY,
MARJORAM OR OREGANO & A
NASTURTIUM BLOSSOM.

SERVES 8.

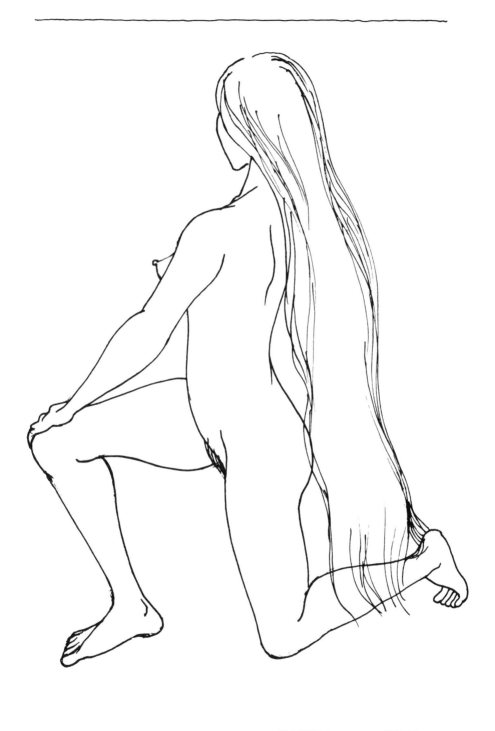

MARINA'S
EGG BREAD

This is a good dough for bread sculpture.

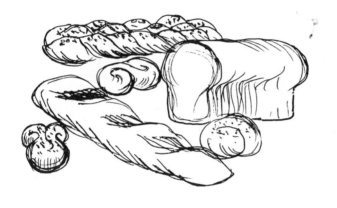

1 C MILK
2 T HONEY
2 T SUGAR
1/2 STICK SWEET BUTTER
1 ENVELOPE YEAST
1/4 C WATER
2 EGGS
5 C UNBLEACHED FLOUR

SCALD MILK, HONEY, SUGAR &
BUTTER IN SAUCEPAN. COOL UNTIL
LUKE-WARM, THEN ADD TO YEAST
WHICH HAS BEEN SOFTENED IN
THE WATER. ADD BEATEN EGGS,
THEN FLOUR IN 2 PORTIONS,
KNEADING UNTIL SMOOTH. COVER
AND LET RISE FOR 1 HOUR IN
WARM SPOT. PUNCH DOWN AND
MAKE INTO LOAVES OR BRAIDS
OR SCULPTURES. BRUSH WITH EGG,
SPRINKLE WITH SESAME OR POPPY
SEEDS. LET RISE 1 HOUR. BAKE
AT 350° FOR 30 MINUTES. MAKES
2 LOAVES.

On the way to Tomales Bay
I saw a lot of wildflowers
called wooly blue curls,
which were filling the air
with their herbaceous aroma.

We had roast oysters and
salad and camembert
and French bread, and
then coffee and a cake
that Karen made.
To roast oysters on the
fire, build a fire of small
sticks, put the oysters on it,
and as soon as the edges
bubble push
them out of the
fire, pry them open
and serve on the
half shell, sprinkled with
salt, freshly ground pepper
and a squeeze of fresh
lemon.

MACARONI SALAD

8 OZ. MACARONI
1 GENEROUS C MAYONNAISE
1/4 C DIJON MUSTARD
1 1/2 LBS. ASPARAGUS, BROKEN INTO
   SMALL PIECES
2 RED PEPPERS CUT IN STRIPS
1 BUNCH GREEN ONIONS, SLICED
   WITH TOPS
DASH OF WINE VINEGAR

COOK MACARONI ACCORDING TO
DIRECTIONS ON PACKAGE. ADD
MAYONNAISE & MUSTARD. BLANCH
ASPARAGUS FOR 3 MINUTES.
DRAIN, COOL & TOSS WITH VEGE-
TABLES INTO SALAD. ADD VINEGAR
TO TASTE. THIS IS EVEN BETTER
IF MADE A DAY AHEAD.

SERVES 6.

109

110

WEIGHT OF 2 EGGS CAKE

WEIGH 2 EGGS (ABOUT 1/4 LB.)
& MEASURE OUT THE SAME A-
MOUNT EACH OF SUGAR, SWEET
BUTTER & SELF-RISING FLOUR
CREAM BUTTER & SUGAR. ADD
BEATEN EGGS ONE BY ONE, &
THEN GRADUALLY ADD THE
FLOUR, BEATING ALL THE TIME.
FLAVOR WITH 1 t VANILLA OR
1/2 t ALMOND EXTRACT. POUR
BATTER INTO BUTTERED,
FLOURED 9" PAN. BAKE AT
350° TILL DONE, ABOUT 20
MINUTES. REMOVE FROM PAN,
COOL & SLICE THROUGH HORI-
ZONTALLY. FILL WITH FLA--
VORED WHIPPED CREAM &
SLICED FRESH FRUIT.

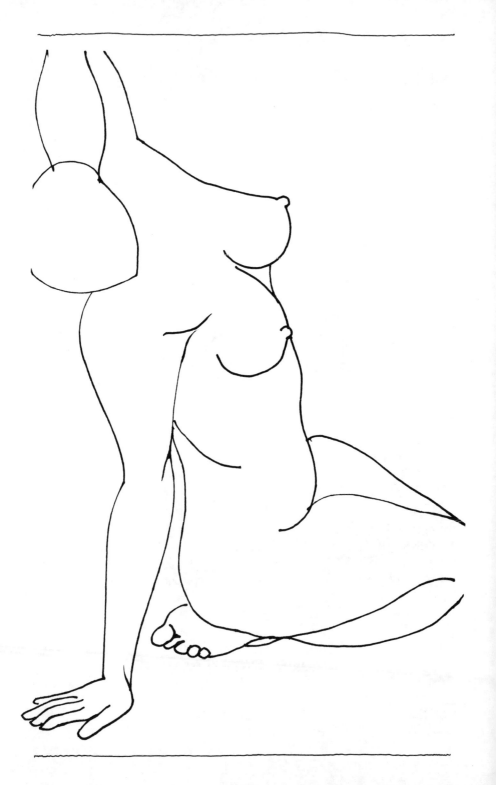

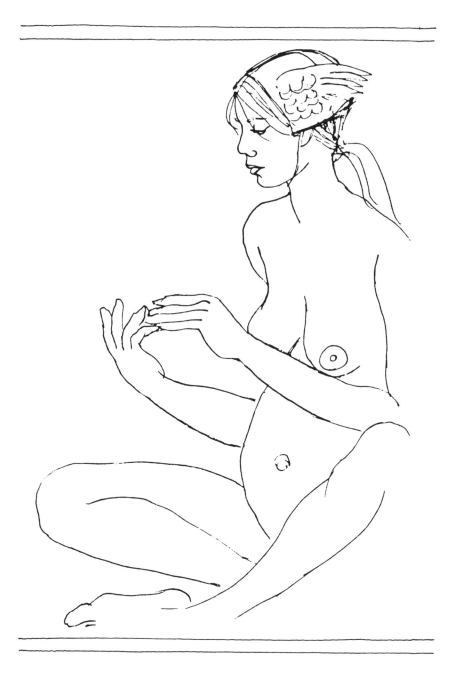

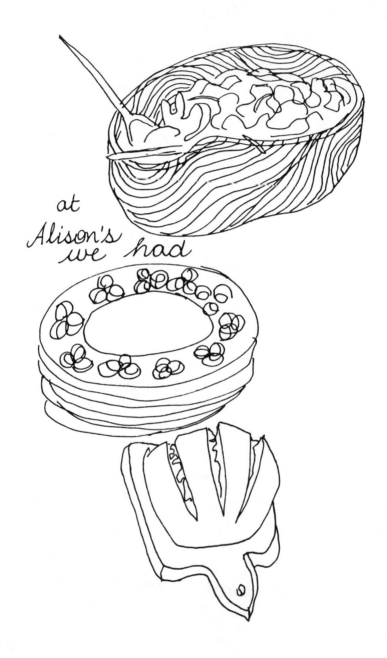

at
Alison's
we had

UNLEAVENED BREAD

2 C WHOLE WHEAT FLOUR
1 C OAT FLOUR
1 C RICE FLOUR
1/2 C PLAIN WHITE FLOUR
4 T SAFFLOWER OIL
2 t SALT
2 T HONEY
2 HANDFULS OF SHELLED
   SUNFLOWER SEEDS
1 C WATER (ENOUGH TO MAKE
   DOUGH MANAGEABLE)

MIX INGREDIENTS & KNEAD
DOUGH TILL PLIABLE. FORM
INTO OBLONG SHAPE ON OILED
BAKING SHEET. DECORATE BY
CUTTING SLITS ALONG TOP OF
LOAF. COVER WITH CLOTH &
LEAVE FOR 4 HOURS. BAKE FOR
1 HOUR AT 350°. THIS MAKES A
HEAVY, DENSE LOAF WITH A
DELICIOUS FLAVOR. SLICE VERY
THIN & SERVE WITH SWEET
BUTTER OR CHEESE.

CASHEW SOUP

1 ONION, SLICED
4 C CHICKEN BROTH
2 C RAW CASHEWS
2 t ARROWROOT
1 T CELERY SEED
2 T COARSELY CHOPPED CELERY
   LEAVES
1/4 LB. GREEN BEANS BROKEN
   IN PIECES
1/2 C SLICED CELERY
1/2 LB. SLICED MUSHROOMS
PINCH OF CAYENNE PEPPER
S & P

SIMMER ONION IN BROTH TILL
ONION IS SOFT. POUR INTO WELL
OF A BLENDER; ADD CASHEWS,
ARROWROOT, CELERY SEED &
CELERY LEAVES. BLEND UNTIL
SMOOTH. LIGHTLY SAUTÉ VEGE-
TABLES IN BUTTER, ADDING
MUSHROOMS LAST. THEN MIX ALL
TOGETHER, SEASONING TO TASTE.
IF YOU LIKE A THINNER SOUP,
ADD WATER. HEAT & SERVE
LIBERALLY SPRINKLED WITH
PAPRIKA.

SERVES 6.

POACHED SALMON WITH DILL

MELT 2 T BUTTER IN A PAN
WITH A TIGHTLY FITTING LID.
ADD 1 C WHITE WINE, 6
SALMON STEAKS. SPRINKLE WITH
DILL WEED; COVER; COOK OVER
A LOW FLAME 10 MINUTES.

'SERVE WITH SMALL POTATOES
AND SALAD: BUTTER LETTUCE,
CUCUMBERS & AVOCADOS.
DRESS WITH 1 T WINE VINEGAR,
3 T OLIVE OIL & 1 CLOVE
CRUSHED GARLIC.

SERVES 6

CHOCOLATE POTS DE CRÊME

PUT 9 OZ. SEMI-SWEET CHOCOLATE
CHIPS IN BLENDER WITH 3 WHOLE
EGGS. BLEND AT HIGH SPEED.
THEN, WHILE BLENDER IS STILL
RUNNING, SLOWLY POUR IN 1 ½ C
SCALDED HALF & HALF. FLAVOR
WITH ¼ C STRONG COFFEE. IF
YOU LIKE, ADD 2 T ORANGE
LIQUEUR. POUR INTO 4 OZ.
RAMEKINS & CHILL AT LEAST 4
HOURS BEFORE SERVING.

SERVES 6.

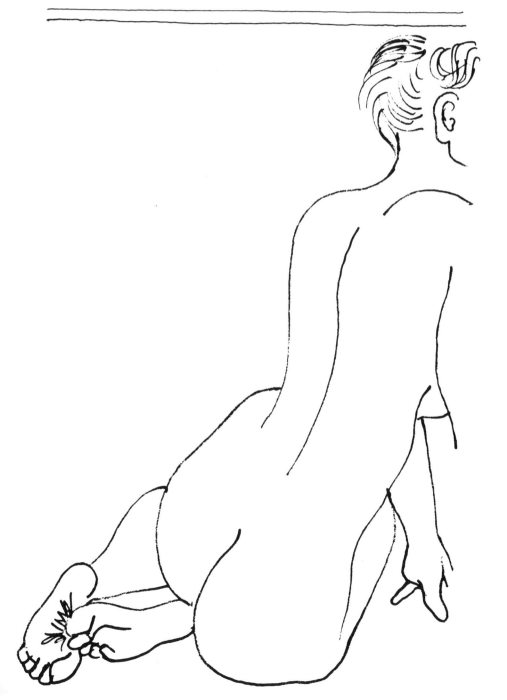

LINGUINI WITH FRESH TOMATO SAUCE

1 LB. LINGUINI
4 T OLIVE OIL
1 ONION
2 OR 3 CLOVES GARLIC ⎫
1 HANDFUL FRESH BASIL   ⎬ CHOP
1 HANDFUL FRESH PARSLEY ⎭
6 MEDIUM TOMATOES, PEELED
MAKE SAUCE WHILE LINGUINI
BOILS. HEAT OIL, IN HEAVY
SKILLET. SAUTÉ ONIONS &
GARLIC TILL TRANSPARENT.

THEN ADD HERBS & TOMATOES.
SIMMER ABOUT 10 MINUTES. PLACE
DRAINED LINGUINI ON A PLATTER;
POUR SAUCE OVER ALL AND SERVE
WITH FRESHLY GRATED PARMESAN.
SERVES 6.

SALADE NIÇOISE

6 NEW POTATOES, UNPEELED
1 LB. GREEN BEANS, SNAPPED
6 EGGS, HARD BOILED
6 TOMATOES
BLACK OLIVES
ANCHOVIES.
STEAM, THEN SLICE POTATOES
& BEANS. ARRANGE ALL ON A
BED OF BUTTER LETTUCE; THEN
POUR OVER IT A CUP OF HOME-
MADE MAYONNAISE. SERVES 6.

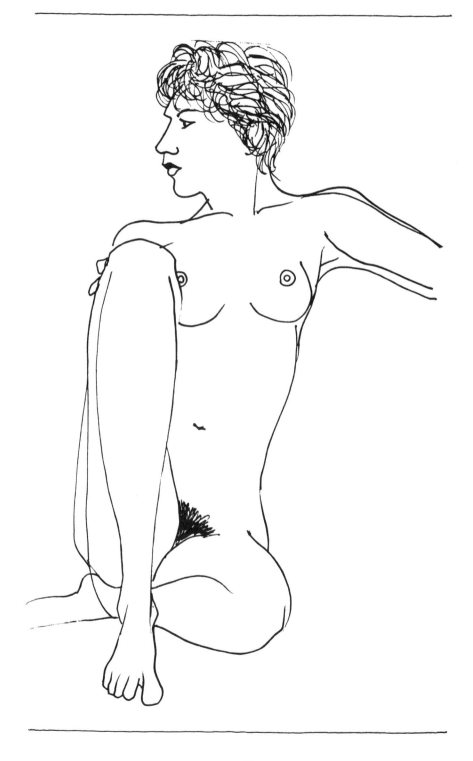

125

FRESH FRUIT WITH RUM SAUCE

ARRANGE FRESH FRUIT ON A
LARGE PLATE. SERVE WITH
RUM SAUCE:
4 EGG YOLKS
1/3 C GRANULATED SUGAR
1 C CREAM, WHIPPED
PINCH OF SALT
RUM TO TASTE

BEAT EGG YOLKS WITH SUGAR;
FOLD IN WHIPPED CREAM. ADD SALT.
ADD RUM TO TASTE. SERVE CHILLED.

128

LUNCH AT LEE'S   11 SEPTEMBER

OYSTER CHOWDER

CUT UP 4 SLICES OF BACON & FRY.
THEN ADD A CUT UP MEDIUM
SIZED ONION & COOK TILL TRANS-
PARENT. CUT UP 3 LARGE POTA-
TOES. ADD TO POT WITH 4 C
MILK. SIMMER BUT DON'T BOIL.
WHEN POTATOES ARE DONE STIR
IN 1 LB. SMALL SHUCKED OYSTERS.
THEY WILL COOK IN A FEW MIN-
UTES. GARNISH WITH CHOPPED
PARSLEY.

SERVES 6.

also Lee served sliced
tomatoes and

WHOLE WHEAT BREAD

4 C WHOLE WHEAT FLOUR
1½ C UNBLEACHED WHITE FLOUR
HANDFUL OF WHEAT GERM
2 T RAW SUGAR ⎫
2 T YEAST ⎬ YEAST
  OR 2 PACKAGES ⎭ MIXTURE
½ C WARM WATER
2 C MILK
2 t SALT
2 T BUTTER

HEAT MILK & BUTTER IN SAUCE-
PAN UNTIL BUTTER IS MELTED.
COOL SLIGHTLY. POUR INTO
LARGE BOWL WITH YEAST MIX-
TURE. ADD DRY INGREDIENTS
GRADUALLY TO LIQUIDS MIX-
TURE, STIRRING. THEN KNEAD
DOUGH ON FLOURED BOARD TILL
SMOOTH & ELASTIC, ABOUT 7
MINUTES. IN A DRAFT FREE
PLACE, LET RISE FOR 40 MIN-
UTES. PUNCH DOWN, KNEAD
AGAIN & SHAPE INTO 2 LOAVES.
LET RISE 35 MINUTES. BAKE
AT 375° FOR ABOUT 45 MINUTES.

GREEK SPINACH PIE

1 ONION, CHOPPED
2 BUNCHES SPINACH, DRAINED &
  CHOPPED
8 EGGS, SLIGHTLY BEATEN
1 LB. FETA CHEESE
PEPPER TO TASTE
1/4 LB. BUTTER, MELTED
1 LB. FILO

SAUTÉ ONION TILL TRANSLUCENT.
ADD CHOPPED SPINACH & COOK
A FEW MINUTES. MIX EGGS,
CRUMBLED FETA, SPINACH &
ONION, PEPPER. LINE A BAKING
DISH WITH LAYERS OF FILO,
PAINTING EVERY FEW LAYERS
WITH MELTED BUTTER. SPREAD
SPINACH MIXTURE OVER FILO.
REPEAT FILO PROCESS WITH
REST OF PACKAGE. BAKE FOR 1
HOUR AT 350°.

SERVES 6 – 8.

PEARS IN RED WINE

MAKE A SYRUP BY BOILING 1C SUGAR
WITH 1C WATER FOR A FEW MINUTES
WITH 4 WHOLE CLOVES & 1 CINNAMON
STICK. GENTLY PLACE UP TO 12 FIRM
PEARS, PEELED & LEFT WHOLE WITH
STEMS ON, IN THE SYRUP. ADD 1C
RED WINE & SIMMER UNTIL PEARS ARE
TENDER. CHILL WELL BEFORE
SERVING. THESE WILL KEEP FOR A
LONG TIME IN THE REFRIGERATOR.

ONION SOUP

4 T BUTTER
4 LARGE ONIONS, THINLY SLICED
PINCH OF SUGAR
SALT TO TASTE
1 C WHITE WINE
6 C BEEF BOUILLON

6 ROUNDS TOASTED FRENCH BREAD
LOTS OF GRATED PARMESAN CHEESE

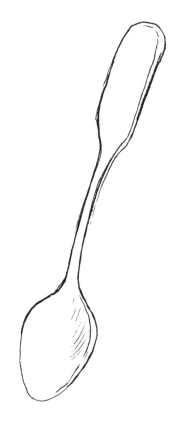

SAUTÉ ONIONS & SUGAR IN BUTTER,
STIRRING TILL ONIONS ARE DEEP
BROWN. SEASON WITH SALT.
SPRINKLE WITH FLOUR; STIR IN
WHITE WINE & GRADUALLY ADD
BOUILLON. COVER & SIMMER GENT-
LY FOR ABOUT 20 MINUTES. SERVE
IN INDIVIDUAL BOWLS, EACH TOPPED
WITH TOASTED FRENCH BREAD
ROUNDS & LOTS OF GRATED PARME-
SAN.

SERVES 6.

TOSSED GREEN SALAD WITH MUSHROOMS & PRAWNS

PREPARE ANY GREENS YOU LIKE.
SLICE 3/4 LB. FRESH MUSHROOMS.
ADD TO 1 LB. COOKED PRAWNS
OR SHRIMP. TOSS WITH THE
GREENS IN A TARRAGON CREAM
DRESSING. THIS MAKES A HEARTY
SALAD FOR 6.

TARRAGON CREAM DRESSING

1 C SOUR CREAM
1 t HORSERADISH
1 HEAPING T DIJON MUSTARD
1 T FRESH TARRAGON CHOPPED OR
  1 t DRIED TARRAGON
2 T FRESH LEMON JUICE
S & P, FRESHLY GROUND

MIX WELL IN BLENDER OR WITH
ELECTRIC BEATER. MAKES ABOUT
1 C.

followed by

CASABA, PAPAYA & PEACH

TOSSED WITH FRESH LIME
JUICE & HONEY.

GARBANZO BEAN PURÉE

1 15 OZ. CAN GARBANZO BEANS
2 CLOVES GARLIC, OR MORE
1 JALAPEÑO PEPPER, OR MORE
JUICE OF 1 LEMON
SALT TO TASTE

DRAIN BEANS; RESERVE LIQUID.
PLACE ALL INGREDIENTS IN
BLENDER WITH 1/4 C BEAN
LIQUID. BLEND. TASTE. ADD
MORE GARLIC, SALT OR CHILE
PEPPER IF DESIRED. GARNISH
WITH CILANTRO OR PARSLEY.
SERVE ON YOUR FAVORITE
CRACKERS OR POCKET BREAD.

CURRIED VEGETABLES

BUTTER OR PEANUT OIL
1½ C TINY OR CUBED NEW POTA-
   TOES, NOT PEELED
CARROTS   ⎫
BROCCOLI   ⎬ 1½ C EACH
ZUCCHINI   ⎭ CUT IN LARGE CUBES
1 SMALL ONION   ⎫ MINCED
2 CLOVES GARLIC ⎭
1 t EACH GROUND SPICES:
   CUMIN
   MUSTARD
   TUMERIC
   CORIANDER
½ t CAYENNE
1 - 1½ C YOGURT

HEAT BUTTER OR OIL IN A
LARGE, HEAVY FRYING PAN. ADD
CUBED VEGETABLES; STIR.
COVER PAN & STEAM VEGETABLES
TILL JUST COOKED. IN A SEP-
ARATE PAN, SAUTÉ MINCED
ONION & GARLIC UNTIL TRANS-
LUCENT. STIR IN SPICES &
YOGURT, BEING CAREFUL NOT
TO CURDLE YOGURT. ADD SAUCE
TO VEGETABLES & SERVE WITH
BROWN RICE CHUTNEYS &
CONDIMENTS.

SERVES 6.

RAISIN CHUTNEY

1 C RAISINS
1/2 C CILANTRO, CHOPPED
JUICE OF 1 LEMON
1 CHILE, JALAPEÑO OR SERRANO,
  CHOPPED WITH SEEDS REMOVED

MIX & LET STAND FOR SEVERAL
HOURS BEFORE SERVING WITH
CURRIED VEGETABLES.

FRESH MANGO CHUTNEY

2 MEDIUM SIZED FIRM MANGOES
1 T GRATED COCONUT
2 T CORIANDER
2 T GRATED GINGER ROOT
PINCH OF CAYENNE

TO CUT A MANGO INTO CUBES,
HOLD IT VERTICALLY; SLICE ALONG
EACH SIDE OF THE SEED ON
THE WIDE PART. THEN
SCORE EACH SIDE, AND
TURN EACH HALF INSIDE
OUT. CUT CUBES OFF SKIN.

INVERT

CUT MANGOES IN CUBES.
COMBINE ALL OTHER INGREDIENTS.
SERVE WITHIN 8 HOURS.

RICE CASSEROLE WITH ASPARAGUS INSIDE

3/4 STICK OF SWEET BUTTER
1 1/2 T CORIANDER
1 T CARDAMON

1 1/2 C BROWN RICE ⎫
3 C CHICKEN BROTH ⎬ COOK
A LITTLE SALT ⎭

1 1/2 LBS. ASPARAGUS ⎫
1 1/2 C WATER ⎬ COOK
A LITTLE SALT ⎭

1 C GRATED GRUYÈRE
3/4 C HALF & HALF

RICE WITH
ASPARAGUS
INSIDE

MELT BUTTER & SWIRL IN THE
SPICES. PUT 1 T OF SEASONED
BUTTER IN BOTTOM OF CASSE-
ROLE, THEN LAYER INGREDIENTS:
RICE, ASPARAGUS, CHEESE,
HALF & HALF. REPEAT, FINISH -
ING WITH REMAINING ASPA-
RAGUS & BUTTER. TOP WITH
CHEESE. BAKE, COVERED,
AT 350° FOR 40 MINUTES.
REMOVE COVER & BROWN
UNDER BROILER.
SERVES 6.

BANANA BREAD

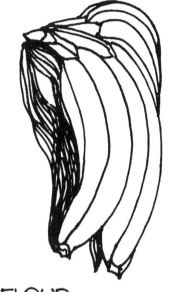

4 BANANAS
1 STICK BUTTER
4 T HONEY
2 EGGS
1 3/4 C WHOLE WHEAT FLOUR
2 t BAKING POWDER
1 t SALT
1 C WALNUTS

IN A BOWL MASH BANANAS
WITH A FORK. MASH IN STICK
OF BUTTER. BEAT IN HONEY &
EGGS. BEAT IN DRY INGRE-
DIENTS, LASTLY INCLUDING THE
WALNUTS. BUTTER & FLOUR
A BREAD PAN. POUR IN BATTER;
BAKE AT 350° FOR 1 HOUR.
STAB WITH A KNIFE. IF IT COMES
CLEAN, BREAD IS DONE. TIP IT
OUT OF THE PAN AND COOL ON
A RACK OR A BASKET LID.

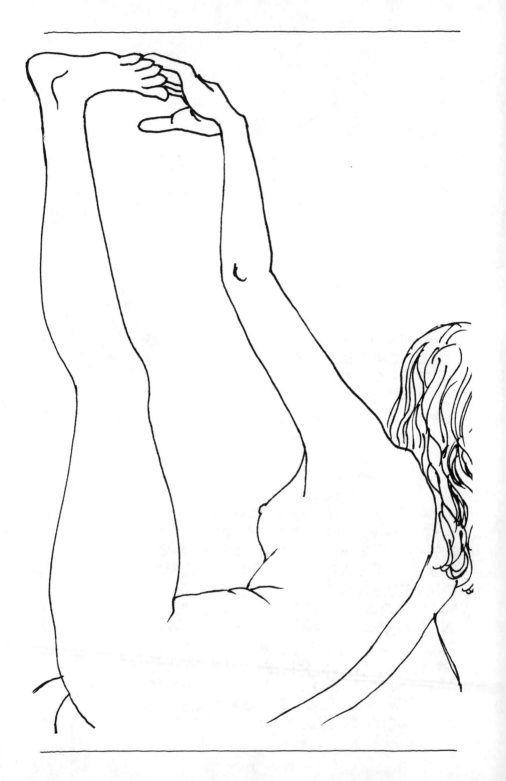

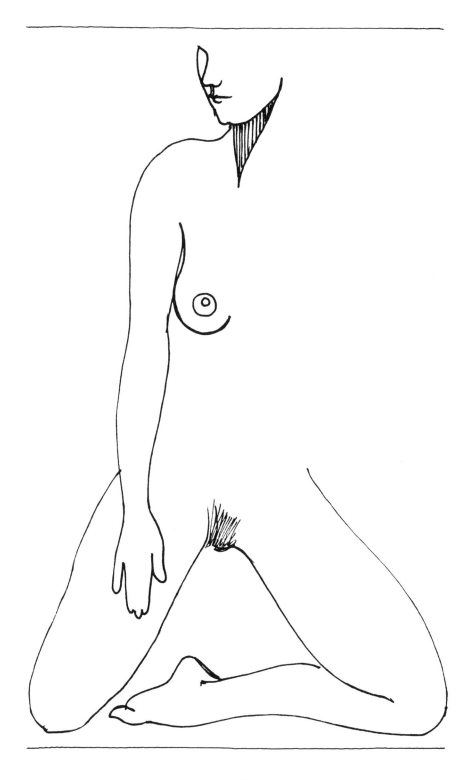

151

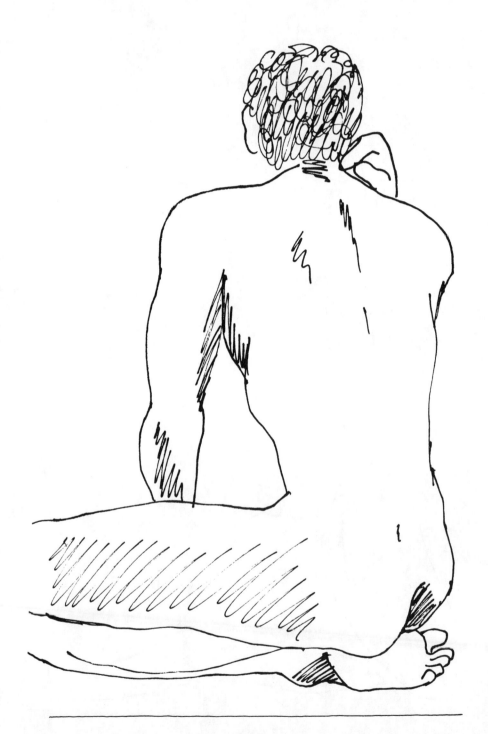

153

OVERNIGHT HOMEMADE LOX

3-4 LBS. SALMON, BONED &
   OPENED FLAT
2/3 C SALT
1/2 C SUGAR
20 CRUSHED PEPPERCORNS
LOTS OF FRESH ANISE (FENNEL)
   OR DILL

PUT ANISE OR DILL ON BOTTOM
OF DISH. MIX SALT, SUGAR &
PEPPER TOGETHER & RUB HALF
OF IT ON ONE SIDE OF THE FISH.
PLACE ON BED OF ANISE OR
DILL. RUB OTHER SIDE WITH
REMAINDER OF SALT MIXTURE.
WEIGHT WITH HEAVY PLATE &
REFRIGERATE AT LEAST 16
HOURS (THE LONGER THE BETTER)
WASH OFF SALT MIX, WRAP &
STORE IN REFRIGERATOR. SLICE
VERY THIN & SERVE WITH RYE
BREAD.

HOT BORSCHT

CUBE & SAUTÉ :

2 MEDIUM-SIZED ONIONS
2 LARGE POTATOES
2 LARGE RAW BEETS
4 MEDIUM-SIZED CARROTS

ADD:

1 HEAD RED CABBAGE, SLICED
2 CLOVES GARLIC, CRUSHED
1 LARGE (49 ½ OZ.) CAN
    CHICKEN BROTH
CHOPPED FRESH DILL TO TASTE
S & P

SIMMER TILL VEGETABLES ARE
COOKED. SERVE WITH SOUR
CREAM.

SERVES 8.

156

PAIN D'EPICE

1½ C WATER
1 t ANISE SEEDS
1 C HONEY
1¼ C SUGAR
1 T BAKING SODA
4½ C SIFTED FLOUR } SIFT
¼ t SALT } TOGETHER
1 t CINNAMON
½ t NUTMEG
3 T CHOPPED CITRON } OPTIONAL
3 T CANDIED ORANGE }
   PEEL

PUT ANISE SEED IN WATER;
BRING TO BOIL & LET STAND.
REMOVE SEEDS & ADD HONEY,
SUGAR & BAKING SODA. STIR
UNTIL DISSOLVED. TO SIFTED
DRY INGREDIENTS ADD CITRON,
PEEL & HONEY MIXTURE. MIX
WELL & STIR UNTIL SMOOTH.
DIVIDE MIXTURE INTO 2 EQUAL
PARTS & PUT IN GREASED LOAF
PANS. BAKE IN PREHEATED OVEN
AT 350° FOR ABOUT 1 HOUR.

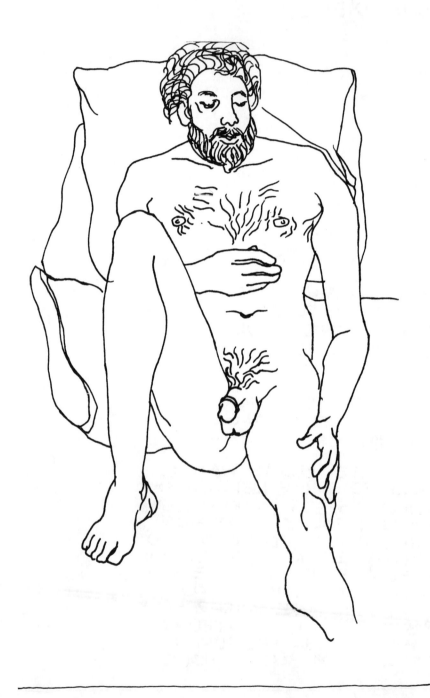

ARTICHOKES WITH
SAUCE MALTAISE

6 LARGE ARTICHOKES,
COOKED

SAUCE
4 EGG YOLKS
4 T BUTTER
½ ORANGE, JUICED
2 t LEMON JUICE
1 t GRATED ORANGE PEEL

MELT HALF THE BUTTER IN
CAST IRON SKILLET, SMALL SIZE.
ADD JUICE; ADD EGG YOLKS
1 AT A TIME, WHISKING. ADD
THE OTHER HALF OF BUTTER,
WHISKING ALL THE WHILE. RE-
MOVE FROM FIRE. ADD RIND.
SERVES 6.

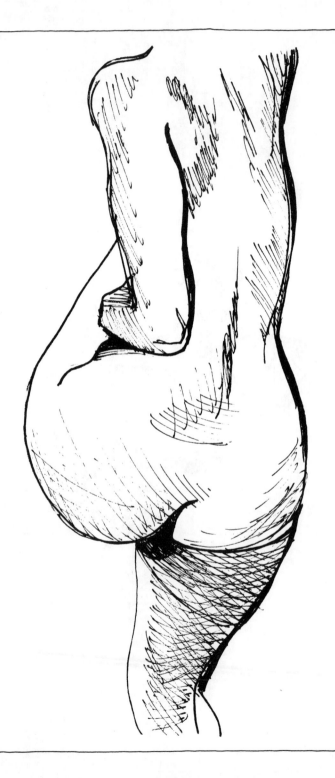

162

RED SNAPPER STUFFED WITH SHRIMP

6 RED SNAPPER FILETS
3/4 LB. COOKED SHRIMP
FRESH HERBS — PARSLEY, CHIVES,
TARRAGON — CHOPPED
I C HEAVY CREAM

SPREAD EACH FILET WITH SHRIMP
AND HERBS. ROLL UP FILETS & SE-
CURE WITH TOOTHPICKS. PACK
SNUGLY INTO A BUTTERED
BAKING DISH. POUR CREAM
OVER FILETS. BAKE AT 350°
FOR 20·25 MINUTES.
SERVES 6.

FLAMING BANANAS

BUTTER
6 BANANAS, PEELED & HALVED
½ C RUM OR BRANDY
POWDERED SUGAR

IN A HEAVY SKILLET SAUTÉ
BANANA HALVES IN BUTTER,
BROWNING SLIGHTLY. POUR IN
RUM OR BRANDY. FLAME.
SPRINKLE WITH POWDERED
SUGAR AND SERVE.
SERVES 6.

AND THEN I STOPPED GOING TO THE NAKED LADIES' LUNCHES. AND  I LOST TRACK AND WAITED FOR

INDEX